IN DISA

A collection of poems, short stories, and letters

JHERELLE BENN

IN DISARRAY

ISBN-13: 978-1523999408

ISBN-10: 1523999403

DEDICATED TO

MY FUTURE
For my children and young writers all over the world who need the constant reminder to believe in the power of words.

MY PRESENT
For everyone who continues to support and encourage me unconditionally on this journey.

MY PAST
For all those who came before me and continue to watch over me.

CONTENTS

LIFE

BLACK BIRD

Wʜʏ ʏᴏᴜ ᴡᴀɴɴᴀ ꜰʟʏ ʙʟᴀᴄᴋ
ʙɪʀᴅ?

This black Bird wanna FLY

late last night this Black Bird threatened
to burst through its cage

behind my ribs

and FLY

Using bones for bass and heartbeat for backline

This Black Bird sings sorrow songs somehow surviving

Wʜʏ ʏᴏᴜ ᴡᴀɴɴᴀ ꜰʟʏ ʙʟᴀᴄᴋ ʙɪʀᴅ?

This world is steady changing. There are dangers on land

 and sky

Still, this Black Bird wanna FLY

This Black Bird dreams of wind beneath her wings

without worry or the woes of the world

This Black Bird

These Black Birds

TOGETHER WE WILL FLY

LOVE

LOVE STORM

They say bad breath stems from the tongue
So I hold mine and keep my mouth closed tight
So you won't smell the stench of these words,
The dark fragrance of my envious convictions.

If I am the Water that flows freely through your fingers
You are the Air that I force from my lungs
And he is the Earth, hardened beneath my feet.
Unlike you I have no fascination with nature's violence
And find absolutely no beauty in the cold, hard, soil.

Yesterday you kissed my face, said everything would be ok.
"We are all nature," you insisted, lifting your hands to the sky
Like a beautiful whirlwind that easily captivated my fluid element.
Dancing within your tornado I showered you with all my love
Water combined with Air needing no Fire to ignite the affair.
It was the rainbow after the storm that caught the eye of Wind and
stole it's form.

The tears fell for countless days and so in my misery, I became the
rain
Flooding many cities while expressing raw rage
Wanting so badly for the Earth to feel my pain.
The damage caused by the storm opened my eyes to the truth!
You are both sweet Air and toxic fumes.
The Earth may hold your interest, but like a whisper in the Air it is
fleeting and thin...
We were fools to think we could ever cage the wild Wind.

THE THIRD SENSE

Together we inhaled the scent of blossoming buds
So many smells between you and I in such a short and lovely time
Closed eyes lead to anxious waiting nostrils
Enveloping in your aroma and the exotic mixture of oils in your
hair
Reminding me of Island Songs, sweet mango, coconut, and
banana.

The smoke of incense burning
Lifting black cherry flavored smoke into the air
Fresh spices, peppers, onions
Diced and chopped for stew
So many wonderful smells were shared between us two.

I imagine the future scents we'll enjoy...
Steamy baths filled with salts, littered with oatmeal, cocoa,
Natural Jojoba beans and aloe
All supplementing our golden brown skin.

Lilacs and daffodils firmly planted with precision line the garden
and all the while sweaty smiling children flit past
trailing the fresh musk of grass and playful youth.

I take you in and my nose is pleased
You smell of calming nature, peace of mind,
fresh sweet bread from the oven with butter and Trinidad
cheese...
You smell of LOVE.

DEAR WOMAN

Dear Woman
I still taste your scent on my tongue like yesterday's seasoning marinating overnight for today's meal.
You complete me in ways where my soul is always nourished.

Dear Sister
Remember when the sun set on our teenage years and met us both with empty wombs and heavy hearts, wondering if we would ever be complete in the way all women were meant to be?
Remember when we laughed all night and fully accepted the judgment of "whores" if it meant we could dance freely and cover up or unclothe as we pleased?
Isn't it such a powerful feeling being a Woman?

Dear Woman
Do you recall the first pull of attraction? Or the first time you awoke drenched and stained red...Your first time being considered a Woman but was there ever a more confusing moment?
I still remember when there was only a father, a son, and a holy ghost fed to me as truth. I went hungry every night confused because what kind of family is ever complete without Mother?
The cross never did symbolize the plight of Mary but when Jesus died,
So did her soul.
She lent her womb to God because he needed her to give birth to his son and yet she is still reduced to just a Woman.

Dear Woman
Is it blasphemous to perceive you as goddess when there is moon and sun in your veins? They are there within you along with the essence of life.
Your worth and value is of such high measure, you are irreplaceable and mighty.

I remember thinking about the world we now live in with female genital mutilation, mass murder of the female infant population, rape, human trafficking, abuse and neglect in all forms of control and manipulation. What about the thriving masculine domination...even the religion my own mother faithfully believed in...and tried to force upon me.

I never really wanted to fear my father in earth or in heaven. I just wanted...love.
The kind only a mother could give.
I actually remember when I discovered that we are more than just Woman.
I remember praying to a God that was a him and a father who I begged for mercy and praised everyday
Truthfully, he's never really had much to say.
But I could tell her everything.
I remember every moment the Goddess was with me
Replenishing
Reassuring
Nourishing
Completely.

Dear Mother
I still feel your winds cool kiss on my cheek.
The cradle of your love lasts eternally
Transforming the cross into an Ankh
Providing spiritual security.
I remember when it finally made sense!
I was learning that recognition of both supreme almighty parents results in a symbol representing true completion and balance.

Mother
Earth
Goddess
Woman
ThAnkh You.

TRIBUTE TO CLITORIS

Imagine if you weren't as lovely as you are
Ultra sensitive and pulsing with anger,
especially when provoked.
You are a hot tempered, attention hungry lust GOD
Who has gotten me into some extremely sticky situations...literally.
But still, you're like my best friend
Been with me since day one...dragged right along through every
rejection,
and every heart broken love story.
You, my frisky companion, have been through it all.

11 years old we were drowning in blood red embarrassment
as my mother proudly informed the entire congregation that I was
now a woman.
I thank you for bearing the brunt of that suffocating diaper like XL
maxi pad
as I sat in the very back of the church shielding us from shame
with the King James version of the bible.
I thank you for not hating yourself as I looked down and questioned
you at 16 years old, confused and self-loathing.
After allowing the first silly boy to put his hand in my pants and dig
for the tiny pink pearl of a treasure that clits are traditionally
expected to be,
let's just say he wasn't expected the whole damn treasure chest!
Upon finding you, all protruding, hard, and massive, he jerked his
hand back with impressive speed and proceeded to question my
sex.
I had no answers and you shrunk away once again with shame.
I hated you. I wanted you to be small, hidden and beautiful.
Why couldn't you just be normal?
I didn't let anyone touch you for a long time after that...I hid you
away
with baggy jeans, squeezing my legs tight to shut you up whenever I
felt you rising.

I scrubbed you angrily in the shower as if one day your size would be washed away and you would hide in between the folds of my vagina like you were supposed to.

But at 18 we fell in love and you matured from annoying and unwanted extra nerves and cartilage into the ultimate power source of my sexual liberation!
You were adored. Padded and prodded, fondled and cuddled
Worshipped with eager fingers
Sucked and tucked into a warm, wet bed of a mouth nightly until you were satisfied and drifted off into a heavenly sleep.

At 21 I began to appreciate your uniqueness.
The way you sometimes poked from my boxers in the morning when my bladder was full and the rest of my body hadn't fully awakened.
Now no man or woman gets past the gates to my heart without your approval!
I'm not being shallow by the way, I just really respect your judgment...
Most of the time...well sometimes.

At 24 I thank you for every experience we've been through together.
Every strange tongue and finger that wasn't manicured and scraped across your insides unpleasantly mistaking my squirming discomfort for uncontrollable pleasure.
I thank you for letting me know right away that I was different...
Special even.
I wouldn't know who I was without you.

DAYS OF OUR LIVES

Monday:
Sometimes she disappears.
Fingers and tongues enter her anxiously, eager to satisfy her
physical needs...but her mind, filled with boredom, begins to stray
elsewhere.

Tuesday:
On the rare occasion they are home together, silence serves as
conversation.
His words bounce off her back like balls on a court as he remembers
when this was a game of one on one and he got to play a position.

Wednesday:
She disappears in my arms, in her words and the pain that was
caused.
She disappears as we make love, even as I bring forth violently
pleasant spasms from her loins...it's not nearly enough.

Thursday:
"Where is our mother?" The children cry.
"Making her bed." Was his solemn reply.

Friday:
She is not here nor there.
We rocked each other to sleep and I was at peace
But I knew by the morning she would disappear.
I slept through the night with her head on my chest mesmerized by
the delicious scent of her hair.
I knew by morning I'd awake to find my stolen lover's smell
just a drifting memory in the lonely air...

YOU COMPLETE ME

Satisfaction
It is the never ending river we swim in at night
Rejection; I'm sick of it.
I'll never dig myself out of this hole
It seems **love** will forever take its toll.
There is only so much I can take so I hope we make this last.
I just want us to last.

If I die before I wake I only pray that I can take our love.
Some say Lesbians don't belong in heaven
So if I die before I wake and I fell asleep in your arms,
I pray that I'll be forgiven.

Are we complete?
Can we fish without a rod?
Must we hide our affection in front of the children?
Or make it clear our intentions are only to love each other
unconditionally
without a solid figure of masculinity.
All I ask is that you satisfy me.

I'll kiss you if they are looking and I will hold you while they stare
And forever until the end of time I will remember
the blessed day I decided to dread my hair.
Satisfaction is the ability to love yourself
and allow another to complete the missing parts of you
that you didn't even know weren't there
If I die loving you tonight...
I hope GOD heard my prayers.

LOVE LETTER

Dear **Friend,**

I only want the best for you. First and foremost, I want to see you succeed. This is my wish for you regardless if you see a future with me. I long for your smile and laughter that fills me with happiness. I cannot even begin to explain the overwhelming feeling of joy and satisfaction I get only when we are together. I want to erase the pain you once felt and even though you are strong, I would like to provide you with a firm foundation.

Dear **Lover,**

You don't want to be hurt again. This I know for sure. The fear of losing your love prevents me from accepting it fully and wholeheartedly. But I would be lying if I said it wasn't everything I desire in a woman. My heart skips a beat when you smile. Your fingers squeeze my breasts while you lie on my chest and it feels like home. Won't you stay for just a little while? Just a little while longer? When I told you that you smell of love I meant it. And when I awoke confessing my love to you in early morning poetry, it's because I dreamt it. Dreams of you and I waking up entwined and the perfect look of contentment in your eyes just as the sun begins to rise. You deserve more. More than I can give and more than you can imagine. The love you crave, you have no idea the power it can hold over you, over me, and over our lives. Tread carefully my love and I will do the same...

Dear --- ,

Sometimes I think you are the fire that ignites the sleeping passions I keep dormant, fearing the chaos and destruction a fire can ensue. And yet I can't stay away from you. You are so powerful in your rage and so passionate in your love. I cannot get enough. I'm not sure if I am scared to hurt you or if the fear is of burning myself. But I am fascinated by your beauty and already surrounded by the flames. I awake every morning whispering your name...
I close my eyes and all I see is Red.

BLESSED AND CURSED

You'd think that when I speak he would listen
The power of my words have gotten me this far
Blessed is this mighty tongue that I speak with
Cursed is the day I fell in love
Blessed is what I am when I wake each day, the breath of life
pushing through my lungs
Cursed is this world that I live in
Where I am humiliated, scathed, mocked, and jaded
not only by the Evil ones
But those who wish me well in the light of the day and curse my
name in the dark!
Oh, how they envy my light and joyful heart
You'd think that when I speak he would listen
Like the anxious ears and teary eyes of those
whose hunger for passion is an insatiable thirst, never ending or
satisfied
You'd think that when I speak he would listen
This tongue has caused tears in little girls who dwelled inside grown
women
Because my *Girl Problems* were their problems too.
I reach inside the chest with lyrical prowess and allow my heart to
confess
the pure truth
This means nothing to you?
You'd think that when I speak he would listen
I command with my voice, with these words I can persuade your
choice
You'd think that when I speak he would listen
Let me anoint his ears with whispers of "I love you"
It would be so painfully true
You'd think that when I speak he would listen
when I scream, "I am blessed! Why won't you hear?!"
He listens with an ignorant ear...arrogant and bold, my silly poems
do not reach him

This blessing is my burden to bear. Words have no power here
And cursed men cannot listen.

SPLIFFS AND SMOOTHIES

We deserve a Spliffs and Smoothies kind of love

We deserve that slow roll of smoke down the throat kind of love

Like clouds settling in a bed, moist with our sweet and salty waters

Lifting, lifting, lifting

an ocean towards the sky

kind of love.

We deserve that banana berry blast

and Garden of eden apple green

with lime and ginger

carrot, kale, and honey

kind of love.

We deserve that turbulent,

"Baby, if we do this it's gonna get rocky"

He said, right before he Rocked and Rolled me

kind of love.

We deserve that kind of love that ain't just about sex

But that pure energy

sparked from the fluidity

of our minds, our souls, and our bodies

healing while connecting

conversing fluently

in their own tongue.

That kind of love.

We deserve that

Haitian Creole meets Trini Patois

Your Voodoo mixed with my Shango

Conjuring magic only we know

That kind of love.

We deserve tutto dolce

Sweet everythings

Together we are always creating

blending two powerful nations

revolutionary

Tribe Making

kind of love.

We deserve that, "Wait, don't say you love me just yet"

kind of love.

We deserve that relax right here on the steps

and smoke spliffs and sip smoothies

kind of love

that "you teach me and I'll teach you"

kind of love

that send you an album a day so you can hear what's in my head

kind of love.

That "For once I'm not afraid"

kind of love.

That connection

That is instant

But we been craving THIS

kind of love.

tantric, electric, authentic, spiritual

kind of love.

The kind of love that becomes ritual

Like, I get more in tune with loving you every day

kind of love.

We deserve romance

That isn't tied to some scandalous sex story

You deserve more than, "He fits the profile"

and a death by gunshot wound;

Sudden and gory.

You my Black King, deserve more

You are Royalty.

We deserve love

I deserve to know that my temple is a place of worship

and when you come to visit bearing gifts you can stay for as long as you wish and meditate in it.

Plant your seeds here, I will nurture, water, and grow it.

I know we deserve this

because the more I get to know you over conversations, smoothies, and spliffs

It became clear that you and I have been conditioned to hate each other.

Powerful as we may be we are disconnected from our history

but still connected to the pain passed down through our ancestry.

Domestic abuse has been common in our families.

We were told what we didn't deserve and eventually it was what we believed.

But you saw the sun reflected in me and my brown skin.

I never saw you as a "Nigga", always as a king.

Somehow we recharged each other's melanin.

We shared words and laughter

Stood silent in an embrace effortlessly communicating

Bonding

Rebuilding

Knowing

We couldn't protect each other then

not during traumatic childhoods

not during slavery

but today,

I can roll your spliff so we can hold a meds to heal our minds.

You buy the fruit smoothies to feed our bodies.

The conversation will flow naturally to feed our souls.

We deserve to know

We don't have to tone down the phenomenon that is Black Love.

We deserve a love that is unapologetic

We deserve a love that looks as simple as spliffs and smoothies

But is the most GODLY union this world has ever seen.

SAFE SPACE

Today he took me on a trip

I say "Took me"

But, I gave myself to him

laid down at the altar

bearing sacrifice

Here amongst the breathing walls

threatening shadows

World's Calling,

"DISTRACTIONS, DISTRACTIONS"

I can find a way to return there with him.

It all started when he left me

and the many words I sought to escape

came catapulting at my face

some felt good

some I had to let it out

Let it out into a safe space

let those tears finally cascade

with laughter and grace

"I'm ok!!!" I screamed

forever amazed by my ability to create

I looked to him and asked,

"Why are you afraid?"

Because the lid had popped off

and the darkness was spilling out

like molten lava cooling I didn't dare touch

just admired from afar watching a masterpiece take form

like lightning that isn't striking

just kinda free falling from the sky

taking it's time

He was beautiful and frightening

Like the end and the beginning.

I wondered...

infatuation or obsession?

Another bystander

romanticizing

battle scars on the eyes

putting people on pedestals

just to tear them down

watch them drown

in this sea of zombies

Worlds calling,

"DISTRACTIONS DISTRACTIONS"

but what are they really talking about?

Not him...or me

because if they dared

to speak my name

those words would finally be worth some gain

some profit

think clearly

you haven't lost it

Let's be honest here,

there were many expectations

dark mass erupting

surrounding

overwhelming claustrophobic-gasms

attempting to penetrate from the inside

But I Remembered his voice...

It's all in my mind

all the words

flooding

staring

grabbing

reaching for some meaning

tryna find it in me

Super Shero

Crunk Chronic

ENERGY Dinero

Electromagnetic waves in these veins

passed through spirits on this journey

Sorry NOT SORRY to say

I ain't in the business of freeing slaves

who think they free.

I know

We all got demons and our own private first class ticket to hell

I'm no longer apologetic or surprised when I excel

I be coming back from a day off

positively re-charged

in the light work part of my life

Trying to remember when I created the stillness of the night

That surrounded us in that safe space in the middle of the day

where we could just be

build and destroy

no pedestals no pressures

no going back

dive in

pull the lever

or pull back and breathe

feel

however you need

just be.

I felt, I hoped, I prayed,

I would never come back from this trip

BUT, because I haven't slept yet

or marinated in it

took the time

to remove myself from the maze of my own mind

I'll say what I've learned...

Well It all comes back to the simplicity of poetry

Oh, I've learned to provide a safe space,

JUST BE

LOVE LOVE LOVE

give it freely like it's free

DEFLECT when deficient

be selective when in need

find a perfect piece of mind

right where I need

right on time

some for him and some for me

I learned it's ok to not rhyme

to feel like everything's not

automatically aligned

random ramblings on the page

that's ok too

alien or predator

The stares will still come like it's a fucking zoo

try and shame and disgrace you

like they ain't never seen power

sexual and feral in nature

uncaged and raw

mesmerized and disgusted by what their eyes opened up and saw

I learned how to return back to that safe space through it all.

Today I took him on a trip

I say, "Took him"

but I'm not sure how it ended

if it will end

if he pretended.

I didn't have any answers

he wasn't pressured to pop preguntas

expected to passively penetrate sidewalk propaganda

or bear the massive weight of the world on his shoulders

at least....that is what I told myself so I could sleep

So I could breathe

I'm sure the trip is over

Now World Calls,

"DISTRACTIONS DISTRACTIONS"

"Why aren't you afraid?"

they're asking

Cuz I have learned to

DEFLECT

LOVE LOVE LOVE

AND

JUST BE

If we journey together again

I am your lover

I am your friend

use the words and time wisely

there is no rush

no expectations

no expiration date on perfection

just BE

whenever you are ready

come find me.

ANTI-VALENTINE'S DAY POEM

I have written many a poem
Poems for lovers, poems for revolutionists
Poems with promising punctuations
Poems pondering prophecies
I proliferate pandemonium with perfectly placed periods
I have been known to conjure powerful prose
With poetry I paint pictures of mountains in nature
Whose arch resembles the diving slopes of a woman's hips
pointing downwards towards heaven
I have been to hell and back in a poem
I have committed literary suicide and literally littered the subways
with linguistics
Dropping poems into the laps of strangers as I pass them by
I have written many a poem.

But this poem feels different
Because I feel different
Today I loved MYSELF harder than I ever thought possible
It is possible to fall in love with self over and over and over again
Today I rediscovered how genuine it feels to be vulnerable
with just this paper and pen.

I have written many a poem
But this feels more like affirmation
Like the Mother Goddess Earth and Universe within me
Giving birth to creation
Casting spells to awaken and reverse mind manipulation
I have written many a poem about oppressed situations
But this poem is my FREEDOM
My savior from eternal damnation
This poem is a self care package gift wrapped and delivered to a
nation of people who are told they must look outside of themselves

for love.

I have written many a poem
Given myself bloodied with ink
Offered up what I know, what I love, what I think
But the time has come to be selfish
The time has come to redefine self-less and give more to self
so that maybe just maybe
When Valentine's Day comes back around next year
We'll all be so abundant and satisfied with ourselves
Nothing will be lacking when it's time to love someone else.

<u>LUCID</u>

LOUD

I like it LOUD
Screaming thunder claps and rips eardrums to shreds
Violent lightning erupts like drums to a rippling beat
We move to the noise
It moves us
Against our will our bodies gyrate to the rhythm
as we glorify the sound.

I love it LOUD
Can't deny the feeling
It's impossible to ignore
We respond with the noise flowing through every bloody vessel
within us
Every joint, every muscle, every bone
falls slave to the noise.

Turn it up!
Add bass, add treble, make it rumble, make them crumble
as we stomp, as we jump
as we make some noise!

I crave the noise in silence
The uncomfortable stillness that haunts us in death
The stifling quiet boredom that kills me slowly from the inside...

I like it LOUD
Bring the noise,
We are alive!

THE BARRIER

Age is the barrier.
A number that places you on Jupiter and I reside on Mars.

Mars: Lights, blinding, flashing from every which way.
The music plays all night. Here on Mars it is always night.
Seizing the twilight hours like nocturnal creatures
We scream from the rooftops, releasing the tension
that haunts us during the day.

Jupiter: Rules and restrictions confine you. You are content to
withdraw to the comforts of your home when night approaches.
Suits and Ties, Suits and Ties
Tight on your throat, they strangle you slowly.

Come to Mars my love
Dance with me on each star in the milky way
I will strip you of your limitations and we will swim naked
cool waves
happy and uncaring.
Soothe your soul as I ease your mind
We'll inhale the smoke of youth into our lungs.
Toil Jupiter's stagnant streets when duty calls
But don't refuse yourself the escape...

Age is the barrier, the distance is great...
Your surety falters...
As the sun sets.

TIMES REWIND

It replaces like a sick dream, a catastrophic display
She was a train wreck, but I'm drawn to her.
It's in my genes, inevitable you could say.
She groomed my ego and stroked my aggressive nature,
She sat on my arm with all her charm
A beautiful disaster, tempting collision.

The clocks have fast forward and rewound
She was utterly alive in the moment I made the decision
to let her be free and be mine
and remain frozen in time.

I am the breath of fresh air from your monotonous routine
You love your life, so live!
Confined in the hells of your very own reality, I seek to free you
From the need to be needed and the pressure of a village on your
back
weighing down the tired soul inside.
We are in the moment, relish in the smile
that slowly comes as you walk through this door
Let time rewind.

And we'll dance. And we'll laugh.
Even though we know it won't last.
The warmth that spreads from your body to mine
as I whisper something delightfully asinine.
And you continue to be inappropriate
Rubbing on my ears..knowing I can't take it.

She's a mess, I'm stressed and we're done here
She's found her way home.
The shifts back in gear and the clocks start ticking.
Sitting alone with myself and I start thinking...
And I came to the realization...I never really know what time it is.

BAD TRIP

The day we met I walked on glass with bare feet.
Not symbolically as a metaphor for my masochistic ways
Literally I shattered empty liquor bottles collected over days.
Smashed them individually against my kitchen walls.
One for every kiss, one for all your scars,
and two for every time I matched your shallow gaze.

The soles of my feet wouldn't even bleed
as I walked across shards of Bacardi and Jack Daniels Honey.
The well had finally run dry.
This explains how even on the worst days I still couldn't seem to cry.
And on that very same day I saw my own pain
reflected in your glossed over teary eyes.

Whether it be glass or burning coals of stone
This walk of shame I'll take alone
and spare your precious damaged soul.

FALLEN
a short story

The temple of the sun was known all throughout Philae, Egypt as a peaceful and religious community. Our great and powerful Pharaoh reigned with a mighty hand maintaining wealth and prosperity. All was in order for centuries. My name is Amunet and I was born a servant. My family has served the temple guardians for as long as I can remember, it was the life I knew. Daily duties no matter how tedious were fulfilled by my family and for the most part we lived in contentment. It has been 50 long years since our temple has flourished. The day our land fell into poverty fear spread like wildfire among the people of the sun. Our Pharaoh mysteriously disappeared with the guardians refusing to protect us. Our sacred chambers were raided nightly by thieves and bandits. Such dark times have fallen upon us yet the strength of my people stems from unrelenting faith and throughout it all we have continued our prayers.

———

One night when the temple had fallen silent with slumber, I entered the great chamber where all prayers were received by the goddess herself. I crept expertly down the long hall that led to the large worship area. Pushing the large jewel encrusted doors to the chamber I fumbled with the satchel filled with my offerings. Even as my back was turned away from the golden deities behind me I could feel the magic and celestial presence like a soft breath raising the hairs on my neck. I turned slowly and took in the pharaoh. He stood elegantly beneath the goddess. I walked towards them bringing bread and jewels (the little I had) and made an offering to her. The energy emanating from the statues seemed to vibrate within me as I fell to my knees and begged for salvation. In the center of the hall just a few meters in front of me the goddess hovered over the pharaoh, her headdress a solid throne.

"Mother of Horus. Protector of children and humble servants. Come to us and revive our temple. The deranged Pharaoh has lost his way and I believe only you can save him. Only you can save us all".

After many hours my clenched eyelids began to ache and I retired to the servant's quarters. The dial of time turned full circle; a new day has begun.

―――

The next sunrise I arose to fulfill my daily duties. Filling large pails of water to clean the temple was among my most hated chore. While walking through the bustling halls I noticed the usually gloomy temple seemed to have come alive overnight. Confused and curious I approached my sister who was partaking in a small piece of bread.

"Amunet, my sister. The goddess herself, mother of Horus has appeared in our temple. She claims to have heard the prayers of a servant and was summoned here to revive our people! Surely she will regain the pharaoh his senses and protect us". My young sister was bubbly with excitement and hope glistened in her eyes as she told me of this magnificent news. Throwing her arms around me we rejoiced.

Could it truly be possible? I thought. The day dragged on as everyone hustled about gathering food, jewels and merriment to fill the great chamber. The servant's duties had significantly multiplied but this was a minor annoyance. Tonight the goddess will present herself to us in human form and there will surely be a celebration.

―――

The temple of the sun had not seen a real celebration for many many years. Even the servants were allowed to indulge in tonight's summoning. I stood amongst a crowd of servants next to my 3 sisters in the great chamber. There was a grand feast and everyone danced merrily. The temple guardians, who had remained unresponsive for 50 years were present. They also believed the goddess would perish our enemies and restore order to the temple. They stood tall behind the golden goddess still, silent, and waiting. My head throbbed painfully from anticipation and perhaps the tightly wound braid my sisters had coiled my hair into.

"You look magnificent Amunet". I spun around to acknowledge the compliment.

"Thank you Ra. Although I would hardly consider these servant's rags to be magnificent". I blushed at the slave boy Ra who has attempted to court me since we were younger. Looking down at my malnourished and skinny body I was immediately self conscience. Luckily the music had stopped and everyone turned to face the goddess. The sun dial indicated the twilight hour; It was time.

We faced the statues and waited patiently for something...anything to happen. Just as doubt started to make its way into our already broken hearts I began to feel a distinct warmth pass over me. A quick glance around at the surprised and confused faces let me know I wasn't alone. The entire temple watched in awe as the shimmering gold melted around our precious goddess and revealed flawless ebony skin. Her almond eyes narrowed as she saw us all staring in admiration. Jet black hair spilled over her shoulders and a sinister smile spread across her face. For centuries the people of the sun were unwavering in their devotion to the goddess and her son Horus, now she stood before us in human form; a miracle in the flesh.

She was all a mortal woman could ever be...and more. They carried her carefully and placed her plump round bottom upon the throne in the great chamber. She was silent and beautiful as my people began to worship her relentlessly. They presented offerings and sacrifices none of which she paid notice. I consumed her with my eyes, her perfect brown skin and the defined curves of her breasts. And suddenly as if she felt my gaze hot on her flesh her eyes shot to my direction and she stared deeply into mine. I fell to my knees alongside my brothers and sisters and began to praise her. She was our savior.

As I lay on my small cot that night staring up at the moon, all was silent but for my sister's low breathing barely audible from the cot beneath mine. Thoughts of the seductive goddess flooded my brain, I prayed for sleep to come tossing uncomfortably a few times before hearing footsteps approaching. I sat up just as two slaves I knew well entered my quarters. One was Ra and the other was a young female who never said much.

"She has called for you". Ra's face was straight and hard, yielding no information. The two waited silently while I hurriedly dressed myself.

We walked down the long hall that led to the great chamber and I looked to Ra my old friend for comfort. What I found was unnerving. His eyes usually bright and hopeful were dull and void of emotion. I looked forward and quickened my pace, anxious to meet my fate.

Arriving at the great chamber the heavy doors swung open and I was pushed inside. I shot Ra one last fleeting glance and finally he returned my concern with a reassuring wink. Then he quickly closed the doors leaving me.

———

The usually bright chamber was suggestively dim with a faint smell of smoke in the air. Struggling to see through the fog, I could vaguely make out a few young girl servants circling my goddess on her throne. They danced monotonously as if in a trance, playing small arghuls and belly dancing seductively. I stood completely still and unnoticed just watching the strange ritual before me. The smoke seemed to come from a controlled fire placed directly in the center of the room. Some sort of unfamiliar shrubs burned unnaturally from the fire producing a thick purple smoke that filled the chamber. After a few seconds the smoke seemed to circle me and force itself into my lungs. I was lifted from the ground as a purple cloud formed beneath me and a playful giddiness took over. Suddenly I felt many things all at once; Happiness, apathy...arousal. I was pulled towards the goddess and her dancing slaves on the lavender nimbus and no longer did I doubt her.

"Amunet". Her voice was liquid gold and echoed throughout the large chamber. I looked directly into the dark hypnotizing eyes of my goddess and knew I never wanted to part from her presence. She held the intense stare while speaking to her servants.

"Leave us" She demanded, and we were alone.

Instantly my rags fell from my shoulders to the floor revealing my small but perky breasts, erect nipples, and smooth olive skin. I stood in my under garments with my eyes closed feeling the smoke cloud my mind. My thoughts jumbled together and I could think of everything and nothing all at once. She stared at my body, taking in every inch of me. I could feel her power tickling my skin like soft fingertips. I opened my eyes and she was upon me. I felt her presence circling my body; the fumes consuming my lungs, the lucid tongue on my neck more like a serpent than a god. I turned to meet my seductress. We stood nude inches apart; me a humble servant to the temple of the sun and the goddess Isis herself in the glorious flesh. I'll never know if it was the mysterious smoke clinging to my insides or the powerful celestial pull on my body, but I began to ravish her breasts hungrily. Her dark nipples reminded me of sweet fruits. As if she read my thoughts a delicious sticky nectar started spilling from the corners of my mouth.

"Your eyes widen in amusement my child. Let the dial of time hold still, tonight time stops for us!" Isis's laughter bellowed like thunder that shook the temple and tore through my small world.

HEAVENLY CREATURES

Every self proclaimed woman possesses her own natural aroma.

Her perfume has a tendency to linger. Sweet Chanel #5 will stay long on the mind but this particular scent, seeps from her skin.

It's the body's natural instinct to purge from the salt of sin.

All the years it took for her to match her shell.

All the compromising positions she found herself in.

Every woman very well knows one intoxicating whiff from a comforting bosom will cause a love stricken fool to succumb to forgiveness,

to surrender to the mighty womb.

I've been that fool.

That gentle lady man.

Feed her when she's hungry, feed her pockets when I can.

Yeah I've been that fool.

I've been love drunk off the scent of a woman.

Thinking a bath in her juices was the only way to get clean.

And in return she was showered with tongue strokes and love notes...happily.

From me, her faithful fiend.

I needed my fix like a pull of nicotine...

The sweet kind...the lovely kind.

But I've learned not all women radiate cheerfulness.

Not all are celestial beings dropped from the sky in a baby powder explosion.

Not all women exude femininity.

Victoria Secret's dream cannot mask bruised knuckles and calloused fingers.

Even CoCo will never be able to compress those broad shoulders or shrink gigantic feet,

the kind where toenails are never cut or painted

the kind that are always rough and blistered because lady shoes made tight and pointed at the tips just rub the wrong way.

I've learned some women smell more like Tommy with less Hill in her figure and more curve in the charm of her smile.

I've encountered some fresh fragrance that seemed almost infantile because the female it drifted from was only a self proclaimed woman for just a short while.

Her past was a smoky trail of self hate and denial.

I've met some amazing women.

And listened to their stories, basking in the musk of survival and wisdom.

And I've inhaled some broken women who I've never seen cry or fully naked in the shower.

Their stubborn stench was dry and suffocating, scratching at my throat.

I've had my fair share of being a fool lost in the smell of a woman.

The surety of her embrace placing me back in an innocent childhood place filled with gentle angels calling me home.

From mistakes I've learned heavenly Dove blended with the pleasant odor of Far Away in a pretty bottle can easily mask the devil in a dress,

Perfectly disguised as love and happiness.

Women are such powerful heavenly creatures.

FIREMAN IN THE SKY

Suck me Soucouyant[1]

My blood is already thin

Your small ball of fire is nothing compare to my burning desire within

My heart hang low and my head held high,

I've felt worse pain than you can inflict

I'm no longer afraid, I'm no longer a child

And I already throw salt on your skin!

So suck me Soucouyant

My blood already so thin

My mommy told me of your evil as we drove to Maquaripe Bay

I searched the sand for stones that might keep the jumbie away

A shiny one in particular matched the clouds, a shade of Earl grey

I looked to the sky into my Grandfather's eyes and it gave me the strength to say;

Suck me Soucouyant

---

[1] In Caribbean folklore a soucouyant is a blood sucking hag who sheds her skin at night, turning into a ball of fire.

My blood is already thin

Your small ball of fire is nothing compare to my burning desire within

My heart hang low and my head held high,

I've felt worse pain than you can inflict

I'm no longer afraid, I'm no longer a child

And I already throw salt on your skin!

So suck me Soucouyant

My blood already so thin

I want to dip my Granny in the Nylon pool and ease the burden of all them years

If the Soucouyant must come and suck something

tell it come and suck away the lonely tears

Let the demon have all the painful nostalgia and leave only peaceful memories

thoughts of only good times

Grandfather was so clever he leave grains of rice for the old hag

about nine hundred and ninety nine!

Suck me Soucouyant

My blood is already thin

Your small ball of fire is nothing compare to my burning desire within

My heart hang low and my head held high,

I've felt worse pain than you can inflict

I'm no longer afraid, I'm no longer a child

And I already throw salt on your skin!

So suck me Soucouyant

My blood already so thin

Soucouyant who lied to ya?

My light it cannot be touched

My family is protected by a fireman in the sky

so if ya think you can burn us, good luck!

Cousin Johann grow to be a good man,

he watch and learn from the best

He holding up strong since the nights became long

and Pops was laid to rest.

Soucouyant ya best go from here before he come to douse your fire

The sun is rising and you're still counting

But your time has already expired!'

Suck me Soucouyant

My blood is already thin

I'm no longer afraid, I'm no longer a child

And I already throw salt on your skin!

So suck me Soucouyant

My blood already so thin

THE GRAVEYARD

The cold earth holds secrets living souls will never hear.

Stepping past tombs and stones,

I read the words etched into forever.

Words dedicated to Toms, Dicks, and Harrys who barely lasted that long.

"Here lies a man. He now rots silently in the ground."

I imagined the epilogue to be short, sweet, and to the point.

The air was crisp around me.

My nostrils flared with the stench of death.

Following my memories with my eyes closed I walk the path

to the familiar plot.

All is quiet and calm. The type of silence only the dead can achieve.

Nothing has changed.

I am here yet again and it seems time has stood completely still.

Unmoving like the bodies lying dormant beneath me.

With the heaviness of my heart, the dirt is parted.

My sorrow is the strongest shovel and it works relentlessly.

And my tears, it only takes a few drops...

The coffin springs open after years of hiding my secrets

I take no notice to the escaping demons; they are no longer my concern.

There she lies asleep.

No peace in this rest.

Falling to my knees...this is the end.

Presenting my gifts and offerings, one by one

they line the marble.

The ring, a promise made but never kept.

The key, to an unknown lock.

Perhaps you knew I would never master the mystery...

Never be able to use it.

A kiss from my lips to the cold hard skin that shows no response

One last farewell.

All these things are gone...And so are you.

Buried six feet under in the graveyard of my past.

PROSTITUTES & MURDERERS

a short story

Smoke from the joint danced in the air. The Galaxy Motel right on Pennsylvania was known for their privacy and tolerance of virtually anything in the special Jacuzzi rooms. So naturally, a blunt was lit and a few bottles of various liquors sat on the end table. It was just perfect for Joey and his guest in room 312.

"You like that don't you? Fucking slut!" Joey laughed, using the back of his hand to slap the prostitute he'd acquired about 30 minutes prior in a local bar and secured for the night with a $50 upfront deposit. Wiping the blood from the corner of her mouth she began to smile.

"Yes Daddy" She giggled. His aggression excited her and so she grasped his hand that wasn't holding the weed and placed a finger into her panties. He returned her sinister smile with a silly grin, taking another pull before dropping it right onto the already dingy carpet and grabbed the back of her neck to reel in a kiss. She stopped him abruptly with surprising force.

"Nu uh uh Bad boy...I told you I don't do kissy face." she informed him. She blew a kiss to the air teasingly and proceeded to roughly massage the bulge between his legs. It was all the encouragement Joey needed and so he hastily unzipped his pants. Using the fact that he still had a firm grip on the back of her neck to his advantage he began to push downwards towards his crouch removing the head of his penis from the hole in his boxers.

"Alright so suck it bitch." He commanded, shoving her face further between his legs where his penis continued to grow from all the rough play. Using her professional oral skills the prostitute pulled him into her mouth first only using her tongue and then managed to

suck his entire shaft down her throat in one smooth motion.

———

Shontelle was excellent at what she did. Balancing college, a daughter, and two jobs was challenging but it never took the smile off her face. The moment Lacey was born they moved to the East New York side of Brooklyn to avoid constant questions. Shontelle could hear the pestering questions in her mind even after they were far far away.

"Why didn't you abort that baby? If you were really raped why didn't you report it to the police?" They would go on and on with the questions and the accusations and the questions all over again.

"When would they all go away?" Shontelle asked herself, moving her head frantically from side to side as if to shake the horrid thoughts from her mind. When that didn't work she began to scream. Grasping her chest for moral support she bellowed from the bottom of her gut hoping the sorrow inside would jump out in the form of her piercing voice.

"Mommy mommy! Wake up!" Lacey struggled to shake her screaming mother awake with tiny little hands. The screaming stopped the moment Shontelle opened her eyes and realized she was having a usual nightmare. Pulling the frightened baby girl into her arms she cooed her with kisses and whispered,

"It's ok baby. Mama was just having another bad dream. It's ok, let's get some breakfast. I'll make your favorite; strawberry waffles and bacon!"

"Mommy why you have scary dreams that make you scream?" Lacey wasn't content with kisses and promises of her favorite breakfast. Even at such a young age she wanted to understand, and just like everyone else she wanted answers. Shontelle didn't have any.

"I wish I could tell you baby." She gave her 5 year old a stern disapproving look "And you know mommy doesn't like questions. Come on and let's wash up so you can eat your breakfast and head off to school and I can go to work". That was that. This was the beginning of a typical day for Shontelle James.

After a bath and breakfast Shontelle helped Lacey get ready for school. An hour later Lacey wore pigtails in her hair, sky blue overalls, and a pink backpack with smiling sunflowers. They were late as usual.

"Come on baby, your teacher said you can't be late anymore!" Shontelle rushed out their apartment quickly pushing Lacey into the back seat of her trusty old Honda and strapping her in. Shontelle made sure to drive just above the speed limit so they could arrive only 5 minutes late. Of course Lacey's stern prune faced kindergarten teacher still claimed this was "Unacceptable!"

"Whatever!" Lacey muttered to herself when she got back into the car "It's freaking Kindergarten..." She looked in the rear view to ensure the freshness of her makeup and then reversed out of the parking lot and onto Atlantic Ave towards job #1.

———

After Joey received the best blow job of his entire life he lay on the bed exhausted. He had ejaculated several times adding another hundred dollars to his expensive bill. The prostitute stood triumphantly before him. She had rid herself of all clothing and was squeezing her erect nipples playfully causing her plump breasts to jiggle slightly.

"Daddy I know you not tired yet. We just getting started" She whined, hopping up onto the bed and kneeling before him. Teasing him slightly she rubbed her hard nipples against his face so he couldn't resist pulling them into his mouth, flickering his thick tongue back and forth. After more suckling and rubbing Joey's erection returned signaling the end of foreplay.

"Come here, Gimmie some of that sweet pussy!" He was rough as he spun her around and forced her onto her knees where her back arched and her backside was raised in the air in front of him. He then began to suck on his left pointer finger using his saliva as lubrication and without warning tested the tightness of her hole.

It was moist and taunt around his finger as he explored her insides. He fumbled for just a few moments with the condom lying on the bed and entered her from behind roughly without mercy. He pounded repeatedly crashing against her buttocks time and time again while gripping her hips with his calloused hands. She arched her back allowing him a deeper stroke, gritted her teeth and moaned at the sweet release of tension. It was pain and it was pleasure, she wanted it all.

———

What a slow and drawling day it was at work. The clients filed in robotically, filled out their intake papers, and lined the seats of the lobby while waiting to be called. Shontelle sat at the front desk with the evidence of how tedious the job really was written all over her face in the form of a practiced smirk. The lobby television told of the usual news; local murders, kidnappings and celebrity debauchery. Just as Shontelle was about to change to a program a little less depressing, something on the screen caught her eye. It was the picture of a man. He was obviously young in his 20s maybe, with a silly grin he must wear all the time on his face. She raised the volume to hear why his picture was on the news.

"We are here live at the Galaxy Hotel in Brooklyn New York where Joe Fontaine was last seen exactly one week ago. Fontaine is just one of the many mysterious disappearances that have occurred in the last few months. As a matter fact, this was the 7th missing person to have last been spotted booking a room at the Galaxy Motel…"

"Deary can you please change the station? My stories are on." It was then Shontelle noticed an elderly Caribbean woman standing patiently in front of her.

"Yeah, sure of course." Shontelle immediately grabbed the remote that controlled the lobby television and switched the channel. Even after the dramatic opening music of "The Bold and the Beautiful" filled the lobby, Shontelle couldn't get the familiar image of Joe Fontaine out her head. Where had she seen him before?

Shontelle continued her daily duties of intaking patients at the clinic. The day moved quickly after lunch and soon it was time to check up on Lacey and head to job # 2.

"Hey, how's she doing?" She asked the young babysitter she'd hired to pick up Lacey from school, bring her home, and watch her for the next few hours.

"She's doing great. I picked her up on time but her teacher sent her home with another note…"

"Forget her stuffy old ass! Anyway, just please make sure you have dinner on time and get her washed and into bed by 8:00pm. And I didn't forget I still owe from last week for staying the extra hour ok? Thanks so much hun! Let me talk to my baby real quick"

"No problem Mrs. James" Shontelle heard the shuffling as Lacey was being passed the phone.

"Hi mommy. I made a picture at school today and I drew you and me and Da…"Lacey's voice faded in mid sentence as she caught herself.

"And who? Who did you draw with you and mommy baby?!" Shontelle demanded.

"Danny. He's my new friend. I know you said not to make friends with strangers but he's 6 years old and his teeth fell out just like mine." At this Shontelle finally breathed, relieved and laughed a little.

"It's ok baby. You and Danny can be friends. Just remember what I told you about making sure everyone respect your space ok? Be good for the sitter and I'll see you in a few hours. I love you".

Hanging up the phone, she grabbed at her chest where her

heart still beat rapidly from the conversation with her daughter.

———

Joey's limp and disfigured body soaked in a pool of his own blood staining the Jacuzzi dead center in the middle of the hotel room. His penis had been amputated and was thrown onto the bed, shriveled and discolored. There were bruises and blisters covering what remained of his body. He had obviously been tortured for hours prior to his death.

Cigarette smoke trailed from the prostitute's hand; a reward for a job well done. It wasn't a pleasant job but somebody had to do it. Somebody needed to cleanse this earth of scum like Joey Fontaine. She scowled as she recalled the memory of him thrusting mercilessly behind her and the unbearable smell of alcohol and musk seeping through his pores.

She sucked the loosey down to the filter and flicked it into the ashtray. Now was the real job. Her cleaning cart was already outside filled with all the chemical cleaners needed to dispose of Joey's remains and restore the room to immaculate conditions.

———

The sun was setting in Brooklyn as the evening went on and Shontelle arrived right on time to clock in at her second job. She worked for a cleaning company that specialized in large corporations, hotels, and offices. She clocked in through the back office and went ahead to the front to pick up today's location.

"THE GALAXY MOTEL; 860 PENNSYLVANIA AVE" Was written in bold letters on the site sheet.

20 minutes later Shontelle stood in front of room 312 at the Galaxy. She had followed protocol by knocking first before using the electronic key to enter, but something stopped her from taking a

step inside. The smell that came from the room was so familiar.

"Come on in. You're late" the voice was a sultry purr.

"Who's there? I'm just here to clean the room" Shontelle stated but obeyed anyway and entered the dimly lit room. Save for a Jacuzzi and standard furniture, it was absolutely empty.

"So we got the Galaxy again tonight. I love it! It's starting to feel like home" Spinning around towards the direction of the mystifying laughter Shontelle faced the mirror. The prostitute stared back at her. She stared confused and angry touching her face where Joey's love taps had bruised her the night before.

"No...." Shontelle whispered to herself and the prostitute in the mirror who just watched devilishly, obviously amused.

"I'm not going to do this anymore! This is wrong!" She grasped at her chest like her very life depended on it.

"Shut the fuck up! You are so WEAK! We've gone through this before. We have to take care of this problem ok. Think about Lacey...There are men out there just like Peter who could get their hands on her."

"I know but..." Shontelle struggled to reason with the angry whore.

"He would rape that little girl with no problem. Men are scum and they must be dealt with. Look at yourself, that sick fuck last night had no problem playing rough neck."

"I can't do this. Peter was wrong, we handled him. We should have stopped then...All those others..." Suddenly without her permission Shontelle's hands began to grasp tightly around her own neck. Looking into the mirror she saw the crazed and conflicted expression as the prostitute laughed maniacally.

"My dear Shontelle, you don't have a choice anymore".

Little Lacey plays quietly with the plastic Barbie dolls that have been laid out for the younger children in the waiting section of Child Services office. She was waiting for her mother to come and take her home. It was a Wednesday so of course they were going to the Cold Stone Creamery where they would carry out their weekly tradition of sampling all the best flavors before settling on the usual mixture. Thinking of the delicious coldness on her tongue made her wish for all these strangers to hurry and retrieve Shontelle. The entire time Lacey was oblivious to the boring news on television. It wasn't until she began to hear some very familiar names that she opened her ears to the words of the reporter.

"This is Larry Truman with 13 News. I'm here in front of Brooklyn's own Galaxy Motel where there has been a series of mysterious disappearances. As you can see behind me the Hotel has closed down due to the death that occurred last night of a young female worker. Shontelle James was found brutally murdered in room 312 this morning. NYPD officials have stated that there is minimal evidence and virtually no suspect at the moment but the case is being fully investigated."

Lacey paid full attention to the T.V when an outdated photo of her three year old self flashed across the screen. Even then she sported the signature pigtails but her hair at the time just barely made the length requirements of the style.

"The now orphaned Lacey-Ann James, daughter of Shontelle and Peter now both dead, has been taken into custody of child services. This little girl has clearly been through a lifetime of tragedy in her very short five year old life. Please contact the proper authorities if you are or know any living relatives. As for the whereabouts of the missing men and what connects these series of unfortunate events happening at the Brooklyn Galaxy motel, that remains a complete and utter mystery".

<u>LUST</u>

LA STRADA ALLA TRISTEZZA

I know the way to sadness

It lies beyond the skyscrapers, past the horizon,

and just between my legs.

There are layers of my mind and a heart that is loving and kind

but take a detour down that slippery downwards slope instead.

The path is curved and smooth

Marked with fingerprints and kisses from strange moist lips.

Intoxicating powered freshness seeps from my skin

giving no indication of the past abuse...

Thrust after thrust after thrust into my hips.

Winding narrow roads leading to a river, once overflowing

with sweet sticky nectar

Juicy dripping mangoes from the West Indies

they have been tasted one too many times.

Protruding and puckered it begs for the sin...Please!

this desire we must satisfy.

Oh I know the way to sadness

It's retained in this vessel

Temple of flesh and worldly temptations...

Sadness lives in the land of no return

hidden underneath pants, disguised with undergarments, thrown into the darkness...throbbing, wet, and impatiently waiting.

Prepare for disdain and despair

once caught in the grip of my swollen genitalia

Bid adieu to happiness

Farewell precious innocence

Adios treasured childhood.

Follow the trail of remorse and self loathing,

Climb shaking knobby knees with rushed force,

tugging my panties aside.

Fearlessly and courageously plunge deep inside

there you will find

true sadness lives.

ANSWER ME

I have questions eating away at my mind

Tearing like a flesh eating disease, why won't you answer me?

Put my burdened heart at ease.

I have questions

Why does it always begin with sex? Why do I always end up here?

Used, broken, alone, surrounded...And alone.

I have questions, you have no answers.

You just take of me, partake of me, this body, my sex.

It always leads to sex.

I am destined, talented, creative, deviant, defiant, stubborn, torn,
denial and alone.

When we are together I am reduced to a gaping hole.

Why?

I have questions like, why am I dismembered and incomplete

Where did it all go astray,

my sense of worth and respect and morality.

How can I regain my sanity?

When does the reconstruction begin or will I continue this path until the end?

I have questions like

How come when I touch you I want to cry?

Tears made from the purest waters of my soul

This fabrication of love, it's a fake but as long as you make me feel whole

it's ok.

So I bring you closer around me, right by me, inside me.

Are the spasms you invoke some sick sinful joke?

Am I crazy? Do I love you?

Will I bare your child, will you infect me?

Will I kill you?

What will become of us two?

Us crazy young lovers.

I do love you...I did love you...When I said it.

When you were inside me.

But I have doubts...and I have questions.

Does your mark leave a stain, will I be scared?

Will you burn me until I am left damaged beyond repair

as a result of our affair.

I have questions that you answer by kissing me on the lips

and cooing me with soft whispers,

brushing up against me, telling me you love me...

Do you love me?

Or am I just another insatiable hole for you to fill?

A WOMAN'S POEM

How perfect is my pussy?

Is it heavenly even when you are not with me?

Even when remnants of memories take your place

Soft kisses laid across your back

The heat of me inviting like heavy comforters in the dead of winter

You only come searching when life has been too cold...

But tell me,

How perfect is my pussy?

When it rumbles and quakes hiroshima explosions

Bringing you to the point of eruption but only when you're inside

on the outside I'm just a side

just a piece of pussy.

Now you wanna tell me how perfect it is

how my pussy is the highest degree of proficiency

how you ain't put the puzzle of your life together yet

but it feels so right when we are connected

then you ejaculate and eject

to leave this perfect pussy neglected.

Tell me,

How perfect is my pussy?

While you're stroking her and humping me...

Is her pussy perfect too?

Velvet pink, sugary sweet...

Does she know the nuances of your likes and dislikes?

Does she do the things I just won't do?

How does it feel to have your cake and eat it too?

Questions I don't ask

Answers I don't wanna know

Not tryna feel insecure

I'm tryna blossom and grow

And this perfect pussy flower

that you been plucking while admiring it's petals

well, it's still gone be perfect

without your second place medal!

RELEASE

When I writhed and stretched inside her I remembered

It all flooded back with the force of an angry tsunami built up from months of frustrated sexual energy

My body remembered

What her skin tastes like covered with my mouth and my essence

What it felt like, raw, unadulterated, unfiltered juicy presence

Everything...she's here now

I feel her...Now touch me

I remember what it feels like when she touched me.

I was coaxed into release at the wonder of her explorations.

I read poetry in the middle of the night

I swam through the womb into the world's oceans singing hallelujah

I only wished I remembered the tune

That sanctified hymn, beautiful lullaby, the refreshing sound of satisfaction

Pleasure and sweet pain combined.

I laid down in her solar system and swapped with red carpets so i could get a taste of the stars

Even if they were just dust on the bottom of her feet

I was starved of affection in a dessert yelling,

"Touch me"

And when she touched me

My nerves were shot and it jogged my memory

Causing spasms to erupt all throughout my body.

When she eased her way in after careful preparation

I needed to feel her rising in me, the hot sticky perspiration

Moving together, hearts sporadic racing

I remembered why humans enjoy this ritual mating.

When she touched me deep and tenderly so

When she rammed me hard and fast I know I'll cling to this memory and never let go

I remembered what it felt like to be beautiful

I remembered what it felt like to be loved

When she touched me in places that I just couldn't reach

I remembered what it felt like to RELEASE.

POEM THOUGHTS

With your fingers inside me

pulling, pushing

I am reminded of the emptiness that once lived inside my womb

the yearning that once consumed those lips you seek to part

Those lips do not speak

despite what you may hear in whispers of the night

Those lips are deaf and mute

You cannot hear them, they cannot hear you.

With your body on top of mine

moaning, writhing

like unsettled tongue in drooling mouth

I am reminded of shadows reflecting darkness

and how much I enjoy being weighed down.

The yearning in my heart to be loved by another

to be wanted, to be dominated.

With my head swirling in a puddle of thoughts

drenched in the morning after Spring rain

still drunk off last night's lust

I am reminded by the peaking buds of purple flowers

That we all take time to Bloom.

METEOR SHOWER

Faster and faster we went

Speeding into oblivion

There was no salvation from this pace

I saw the ripples on her skin when I closed my eyes so I told her,

"I can see you're determined to win this race...But we're going to die. And it's just a pity that you're so pretty...Beautiful even.

My blood boils and centers in my core at the very mention of your name.

This isn't a fucking game!

We are two meteors propelled towards each other.

And when we finally collide, we are going to die."

The attraction was intense and I didn't really know why.

She tunneled right through my defense because I wanted her inside.

I wanted her inside me while I was inside her

Imagine the magnetism between two meteors drawn towards each other.

The result will be fatal but faster and faster we go

The faster and faster we push until the pressure causes us to explode and she falls asleep in my arms

I thought I was the one with the charm...But she is a star

Burning brightly and shooting in my direction at 157,000 mph

Faster and faster building speed and power

I love her but I'm afraid there is no way to prevent this meteor shower.

THE AFFAIR

The broken shards were so red as they cut through my chest...Erupting inside my rib cage.

Thousands of crimson fragments shot through me over the most miniscule things in life.

And I smiled...Heartless as I was, it was pure freedom!

Free to roam the New York filth without getting so much as a spec on my shoe.

Without a pulse my lifeless heart bled all my tears in the sewers of Brooklyn.

Pure freedom! Free from the painful irony of love

Until...I read your words.

When you painted your soul with those words my lungs inhaled so deeply

I felt air for the first time.

inhale and exhale slowly as your pen scribbled those words

and my heartbeat in a way so unfamiliar...

With every word you wrapped a lyrical finger around my bloody, lifeless corpse of a heart and rejuvenated all I thought would remain lost forever.

With every word you ignited the fire in my empty vessel and gave fuel to the affair.

Each letter brought me closer to humanity

Each sentence reminded me why I ever loved to begin with

And now I am truly free

Without speaking a word you have mended my broken heart.

ROCK GOD

While they wonder

heads are left hard and empty

They are wondering about him

digging graves with their perceptions

begging to know and see how we survived the witch hunt

The spells he cast how good they must be

You have no idea!

First of all,

It's not a pedestal, it's a mountain he stands on

When you shape your mouth to say his name

make sure your throat feels the hardness of the G

and the vibrations rumble throughout your body on the OH!

and trust you won't ever forget that D.

He saved me pounded my insecurities into a bloody pulp

got you standing outside the door worried

if you will ever see the old me again

you won't.

Secondly,

You can't demonize what the world has already tried to cast into the darkness

He has survived it

then he threw me a lifeline

I didn't even know I was drowning

I didn't even know how much I needed his loving

and you will never get in the way.

His love is a runaway train speeding off the railways

coming straight towards me

and I'm not worried...So why are you?

I know the sight of such high general aptitude has twisted many minds

leaving fools confused by my dude

but he's only rude to you.

Me?

I be his sweet sugar plumb patiently waiting for him to test my ripeness

I be his groupie, screaming his words at the world

because his music more than moved me

He took me away from the pain in my own back just for a moment

and when I got back I was his lawyer

defending him against the scummiest of prosecution

you'll have to get through me if you want an execution

I'll be his submissive

covered in his scent

collar round my neck so he can lead me to what's next

I be his muse

hands bound, senses muted

ass sore, propped and tooted

so them heavy hands can land just right

yeah I be his target

Because sometimes we like it rough

But I also be his healing

With me he don't have to act tough

I be his Freedom

and I know they are still wondering

but don't you worry silly mortals

There is lots more to come.

<u>LIFE</u>

EARL ST. CLAIR CORNEILLE

How can you define a year?

12 months of grievance

Tears that stained our faces and hearts that were heavy

365 days to long for your familiar embrace, crave your reassuring
voice, and miss your love

Wishing you were here with us to share these precious moments...

This was never easy

We have often cried; shed tears of a family whose great and mighty
tree has died

And now we honor you

Who fought the flames; evading burning licks of danger and proved
yourself a hero

You saved us all

Father, husband, leader, and friend

You bravely battled the inferno

You were a protector; a solid rock or wise stubborn horse who
refused to heel

You taught us the lessons we needed to survive

Our forever beloved and dearly missed,

Earl St. Clair Corneille.

DEAR GRANDFATHER

06/20/2011

For a long time I've been meaning to write you. It was very difficult because I usually write very impersonal and structured essays or indirect lyrical poetry. Now that I am nearing adulthood and you have fallen very ill, I feel like there's no better time than the present to say all that needs to be said.

I haven't been free writing as much as I used to. It feels so strange not being able to express myself through writing but the stress of living on my own has really been a burden on my creativity. Whenever I try to write from the soul or let things come naturally I end up stopping halfway through and re-writing the whole thing. Maybe it's because I'm getting older, or maybe it's just because I wrote so much in the past that I've used up all the words there are to say.

One thing I love almost as much as writing is acting. I wish you would have been able to see me on stage. I recently performed at a theater festival in Baltimore with my school and I can truly say it has been one of the most exhilarating experiences in my life. I found a new love for Shakespeare and I hope to be on Broadway one day.

I wish you were able to come stay with me for a week or two in New York. Although I didn't grow up in Trinidad with the rest of the family and learn to cook real Caribbean food, I did learn to cook a few things. I taught myself to make curry, stew, bbq and baked chicken. I also learned to make country fried steak, pepper steak, biscuits, ribs, king fish, macaroni pie, and a bunch of other things that I cook for dinner. I like to bake a lot too (just not from scratch like Grandmother). Everyone loves my red velvet cupcakes. I also clean a lot more than I used to growing up. Every Sunday I wake up early so I can clean the whole house starting with the bathroom and make lunch.

I just wanted you to know that I'm still the crazy Granddaughter who ran from you in the airport just for the sake of running. I'm still the same Granddaughter who probably destroyed more things in your home than you can even remember. But I have grown into an adult who understands priorities, responsibilities, and hardships. I'm still learning while living life and trying to stay sane. I'm nervous....

——

My Grandfather passed away a few days after I began writing this letter. I never got to finish and he never got to read it.

MAY

Yesterday. The past...Redundant words circling my conscience.

Walking with my head faced towards the ground, I am lowly.

These words that push me further and further until I am no more.

Nothing: that is me and no one around says any different.

As my gaze meets the floor, I notice peculiar things...

Leaves fallen from glorious trees. They are crumpled and defeated, ripped from the comfort of a home.

Moisture collects dampening the remaining shredded and ugly pieces.

I stare at my companions; leaves plastered to the concrete.

We are one with the earth, disconnected from this world where no one bothers to look down...and yet they look down on us. They look down on me.

The crowd appears. They are faceless sheep with high heels and glistening shoe shined hush puppies. They are monsters in their judgement and harsh words.

You shiver in the wind and I long to comfort you. To scoop the bits and pieces left intact and carefully carry you home in my shallow pocket.

Sneakers and boots. They mark you and crush you...Holding you down, keeping you there. I watch in silence.

Today when I return there will be no leaves. The cold empty ground will yield no fragments, no evidence of your existence.

I will lay in your place. They will walk on me, keep me down as they always have.

Invisible to the bustling herd, I am submissive to their abuse.

Complacent in my position I stare up at the sky...at the outstretched branches with an abundance of thriving emerald leaves.

Today I will surely die. They will trample me with their open mouths and closed minds.

Tomorrow I will be reborn, resurrected healthy and green...

Looking down on the world, and above it all.

HOPE

Hope came

on a Wednesday

in the middle of the day

just in time

just in time to remind everyone

that even without the trimmings and lace

life is a gift we can unravel every day

Hope came

in the middle of the year

bringing that lesson and other gifts

Hope came pulled by the moon and sun kissed

with a name so strong

Mother added extra letters on the end to soften it

But still,

Hope came hard

plopped out

in the middle of her siblings

while forcing out the last bit of what she didn't need

right there in front of everyone

And still,

to this day

Hope has no shame

She spills her life and purges on stage

Still hoping to truly connect and inspire

allowing her heart and mind to conspire

born with healing waters flowing

and the fire of a revolution

burning inside her

That little girl who wanted to be an inventor

so she invented stories

where the people in her life transformed into the heroes

she knew they could be

That little girl who believed in magic

because her mind altered realities on the daily

Hope was Born Free

She came

She came

and she's here

still living

inside me.

3 GENERATIONS

Douglin

Edna bore her beautiful brown child in a town named for royalty.

They were the children of Kings and Queens, children of slaves, now children of the colonies.

They were beautiful and brown and their world was small and naïve.

With only one station to choose from British news droned from the radios and by the late evening the MUSIC came.

The 'ting ting' of Steel Pan and shake of Maracas.

The Boom Bang of Congas and Bongos told their stories and calypsonians sang their troubles.

The soul's language poured into jazz, rhythm, and blues while generations of culture intertwined with harmony and it was heard clearly above the noise of colonization.

Brown baby girl danced to her soul Music and learned to absorb the Caribbean sun into her flesh so that she could one day offer her womb to replenish the earth and the stories would never be forgotten, the culture would always survive, and the Music would travel through time and across the sea, an immortal reminder of her people's power and beauty.

Brown baby girl grows healthy and strong. Now she is woman with hips and curves.

Sharp tongue to lash, Sharp mind to get what she wants.

Soft hands to nurture, strong hands to knead dough for dhalpuri and dumplings.

Precise hands to bake fresh sweet bread, to cook well seasoned salt fish, chop onions, mix spices, fry bake, sweep, mop, and scrub.

She is proud and radiant as the strength of the sun shines in her heart and the blood of royalty flows through her veins.

Smallie

A queen is born in Princes Town.

She is the first born and the first to taste the freedom of independence.

History will remember war, the presence of American military bases, empires, and federations.

A young brown queen remembers Chaguaramas and Arima. She remembers the magic of Music evolving, expanding, and diversifying from calypso to soca to chutney and parang.

She remembers Coney Island adventures and love letters written by the roughneck Vinci man from Laventille who stole her heart.

She remembers carrying the Caribbean sun over the waters and harnessing it's warmth as she took her first steps on cold American soil. She remembers the harshest winters of her life spent in a foreign land.

She remembers the pull on her soul as she returned to her homeland to bear the fruit of her loins as if Eric Williams, father of the nation himself was calling her home.

Jan Jan

Born in the Port-of-Spain and brought to Bon Air gardens to blossom like the exotic black flower she was. The Music in her soul could be heard all through the town and it was clear she was special. She was life. She was everything. A magnificent black diamond.

Liquid gold left in the sun to harden and polished smooth with cocoa.

She was three generations of eminence placed into a single heart and forged with everlasting love.

She stood tall as any man with the strength of an entire nation and the sun shone brightly within her illuminating the sleek charcoal skin that stretched over powerful bones.

She danced to her soul music as her mother did and her mother before that.

They were the children of Africa. Children of Kings and Queens, children of slaves, children of the colonies. Children of the Sun.

Their stories will be told, the Music from their soul's will forever be heard a deafening echo in the ears of their oppressors.

The culture will always survive growing stronger and shining brighter with every sunrise.

WITHOUT I

Without "I"

Can "you" relate?

Feel "me"

with the weight of trembling fingers scratching away at an unfinished poem.

Without "I"

Could anyone understand and comprehend?

Absorb the sensations these words express

from one human to another

a beating heart's rhythm heard loudly over all the calamity on this earth.

Each ear individually satisfying an insatiable thirst for familiarity, like-mindedness, current events, and kinship.

Without "I"

Without this general proverbial "we" or that lonely forgotten "us".

Without directly relating or meaning exactly what you're saying, being concise or implicating…

Without "I".

Outside of oneself lies everyone else; a world worth exploring.

Narcissism is only at the tip of loneliness

so it's easy to place "I" at the center and project.

Everyone else is the problem.

I am, I will, I won't, I do, I don't

I need I need I need I need

Geez! Is there any other way to start a sentence?

To describe, to interact, to confess?

Is there any other way to secure happiness?

Would "they" understand, Would "You" die

If today for once, "We" didn't think about "I"?

SIMPLE SOLITUDE

Simple Solitude brings thoughts that flow downstream with the river and takes time to rest

And memories that live in the many years that have past

Memories that lack the power to haunt and terrorize

They are more like demons with a treacherous agenda

They are more than words that flash back and dreams turned nightmares resulting in gasps for air in the middle of the night

The desire is painful

The wanting and yearning to past the time, increasing the distance between now and then.

Simple existence

Love in its truest form is innocent simplicity

A kiss that gives life to butterflies strong enough to survive the stomach's acids

Who only flutter when true love is present

Fairytale childhoods before molestation and perversions, suicide attempts, abandonment, accompanied by lonely silent darkness

Before life became a job

Before families forced their children into closets

Before complexity meant excitement and different was no longer beautiful

Before laughter was burdened with the threat of tears

and sadness could no longer be cured with ice cream and a loved one's blanket of safety

Or a strong embrace

Tomorrow then, was just the day after today.

Simple Purpose

Simple Words

These complicated moments are so unhealthy

I miss the simple things.

LOOK AT THESE HANDS

Look at these hands.

Lean and strong.

See how they are scarred and rough.

See how everything they've touched is now in pieces?

See how everything these long fingers wrap themselves around end up broken, or slightly damaged and bruised.

Look at these hands how they have used and abuse.

See the lines indented in this palm and read the stories they trailed from.

In the beginning they were small and soft reaching for a mother's love like a blanket in the winter.

But mommy could never protect us with her own hands so nights were always cold and bitter.

In the beginning they were gentle holding fathers hand and trusting him to lead the way.

He took me to the darkest places and showed me how to hold the person you love so tightly and with such force they are bound to break.

Look at these hands.

See how they strangle?

Any chance for real love is suffocating, gasping for air.

I don't know what love is.

I remember it vividly the first time my daddy showed me how to love.

And the blood my mother shed while she accepted it and I remember how it felt to not be able to use my then tiny shaking hands to defend her.

She called for my help told me to run and if for that instance I only had a gun I swear to you that man, my father would have died that night by my hands.

Is that what love is?

These two hands now all grown up wear self inflicted scars, bones that were bent and never mended, a broken promise ring ironically stirring up memories of infidelity and a trail of broken promises.

I remember the first time these hands gripped the blade and slid across my wrist breaking skin.

I remember the struggle and every losing battle to the demons within.

I remember what it felt like to cut myself down and then pick up the bloody shards one by one piercing my finger tips.

Is that what love is?

These hands that envy the caged bird and its ability to sing. Everyday I live in chaos with these hands that somehow destroy everything. I grew with a wounded voice and learned to keep the songs of pain to myself because they never made me feel free.

In some ways I'm still trapped in the darkness silently watching mommy and daddy make what I thought was love.

And now I have become the nightmare.

Cursed with my father's hands, these demons are my inheritance and they whisper louder than any prayer.

They tell me I don't deserve to live and sometimes I believe them.

With a not so green thumb these hands plant seeds that are crushed before they can multiply

These hands consistently thwart any possibility of normalcy in this fragile life.

Look at these hands,

look at me!

Scooping up the pieces of a broken home

Fighting the demons oh so quietly

I will chop these hands off if I have to

I don't want to break the things I love anymore.

Daddy, I'll die if I end up just like you.

CAUTION TAPE

My body is a crime scene that reeks of intrigue but trust me you
don't want to get caught up in this murder mystery
I have slain fragile hearts in careless abandon/been unfaithful, been
unkind, broke promises, spoon fed lies
Many times women have died, their hearts crushed/ I do not deny/
It was I who committed the crime

You deserve to be loved without distractions and accepted without
exceptions
This isn't a rejection but a warning for your protection
My heart is a bloody crime scene and I advise you to proceed with
caution

Curiosity killed the cat / it had 8 more lives to come running back
but even small minded creatures can learn from their mistakes
I want to prevent you from making one and save you a life
It may come in handy when you decide to go lurking in the night

Just be sure to stay clear of restricted areas

GIRL PROBLEMS

Girl Problems, Girl Problems. Yeah Yeah Yeah.

I got Girl problems, Girl problems. Yeah Yeah Yeah

I'm looking at you staring at me and I start blinking rapidly.

You love my eyes.

You don't see how they can detect the lust and the thirst right under the smile.

You don't see how these beautiful eyes can no longer cry.

As a woman I've had trials and tribulations, been raped and sold to the world.

Judged by what I wear, classified after only physical observations

were made.

Yeah I'm blinking and I'm cute but you'd prefer if I was mute because you don't wanna hear what I gotta say, I'm just a chick and it's a man's world at the end of the day.

Girl Problems, Girl Problems. Yeah Yeah Yeah.

I got Girl problems, Girl problems. Yeah Yeah Yeah

See the reason I'm blinking so sensually and frequently is

because my eyelashes have been coated and pulled,

curled upwards to compliment my almond shaped peepers...

They are extremely heavy.

And sometimes the eyeliner cakes up and so that day I won't wear any makeup

but the mirror says I'm too plain.

And Society says I'm too skinny

A few years ago I was too thick, now I'm chasing dreams of being a bad bitch

learning how to play on my own insecurities because of what the media constantly depicts.

Girl Problems, Girl Problems. Yeah Yeah Yeah.

These are Girl problems, Girl problems. Yeah Yeah Yeah

In the 60s they wanted a silent housewife. Today I better make my own money If I wanna take the role of "wifey".

The standards for women have changed

but the sexist mentality has remained the same.

We are treated as toys, lesser beings, property, or things.

But not all of us are ditzy and distracted by shiny diamond rings.

Not all of us are content being lied to and abused

by the same knight in shining armor who's supposed to save you.

Some of us are stronger...But we all got issues.

Girl Problems, Girl Problems. Yeah Yeah Yeah.

I got Girl problems, girl problems. Yeah Yeah Yeah

What's the most amazing is I relate to the fellas too.

Yeah I chase pussy too.

In the pursuit of her juicy fruit,

I'll spend money; I'll spend time in an extravagant gesture.

Go the length or the mile, for a woman I'll take any measure.

And when she lets me in, beneath and between the warmth of her soft skin

I'll make sure she is pleasured.

I love the scent of a woman and it's sweet tickle in my nose; sneeze.

I take my time cause she's classy but I'll sneak between her knees with a lesbian's ease.

I'm a slave to my desires, mesmerized by the things that they do.

They draw me in with the same spell they cast on you.

See I can relate, I got boy problems too.

Girl Problems, Girl Problems. Yeah Yeah Yeah.

I got Girl problems, Girl problems. Yeah Yeah Yeah

THE LAND OF THE YOUTH

We are told mistakes from our elders,
Painful memories my daddy don't want for me.
How dare they forget once dancing in our place; liquor burning,
bodies writhing, soft whispers, loud moaning.
To be young is to be free!
The land of the youth, the land of the youth; we are living in the
land of the youth.
It's an old man's utopia he can only wish to see again.
Utopia...the escape we hungrily embrace as the rush makes it way
from the nostrils straight to the sky, pass that spliff so I can keep
this high.
It is clear I've had my fill but I am still ever so careful not to spill a
drop of this drink. More alcohol I could never refuse.
I'm living in the land of the youth!
Worried and aging souls shed tears for us; praying on tired creaking
knees for our salvation.
Jesus will return they say to rupture this blasphemous nation.
But what my Christian Mama can't see is my piss reeks with the
stench of Hennessy.
And I'll only ever pop a purple ecstasy.
Her message falls on a deaf man's ears.
Narcotics replace doubt and the deepest fears.
I live a life without limitation, liberated from suffocation,
Rules, norms, regulations.
I'm living in the land of the youth!
The land of the youth, the land of the youth, we're living in the land
of the youth.
So what's another shot, sniff some shit why not?
Let's dance forever and never stop,
As long as someone rolls a blunt
Because I gotta have my pot.
I'm living in the land of the youth!

FUEL FOR THE FIRE

We love to dance in flames, and feel the lick of the fire.

Drink more than our fill and smoke to get higher, escape from our problems is what we desire

But what will we pay when this precious life is draining away and the cost is oh so dire?

Drink your sorrows and swallow the pain intoxicate with vodka, self medicate with rum to forget who you are tonight and ask yourself tomorrow if you like what you've become and that's only if only you remember what you've done.

This is Satan's world and he'll hand you the bottle and watch you speed to your death full throttle.

A complete disaster, keep going you're on a roll and he's running the show

There is nothing worse than the illusion of control.

We love to dance in the flames just to feel the heat just to feel at all

So we overdose on what we know as good kush and alcohol and tell ourselves we're gonna go out and ball

But there is no hope for you in that bottle; your sins are stains the liquor cannot wash away.

Black outs don't work the same as white out when you put them on your mistakes

You can turn the lights out but the problems are still there

they aren't completely erased even after straight shots after shots you make sure not to chase.

Shots, shots, shots, after shots shots shots!

Everybody! Go ahead and keep on the thinking the party won't ever stop.

Test your limits, drink until the anguish in you begins to churn

Oh how we love to fill ourselves with flammable liquid and dance in the fire to feel that slow burn

just looking to feel anything at all that will satisfy this yearn.

Keep searching for happiness in that bottle, one day you will reach the bottom...one day you will learn.

WE GOTTA SAVE OUR YOUTH

It was the realest moment when my youth said he hates police brutality

Cause I've been put behind bars just for spitting this poetry

That truth wasn't meant to stop you from speaking your mind

But to remind that his problems are the same as mine

See Brownsville be the hood my friend Matt got stabbed

And where they jumped lil Vickie right on Sutter Ave.

Every morning take the 3 train to Rockaway

Wondering who I might have to fight to save my life today

The truth is I never fought I'm not a savage like they say

I elevate to feed my mind and keep above the fray

These hoodlums aren't our enemies none of us chose this way

But here's a lesson on conditioning

What we were taught back then still applies to this day

And we were taught we weren't humans and our skin got us slain

So I return to Brownsville to teach how poetry saves

We gotta save our youth

A city with no youth is like a car with no gas or a cup with no juice

it's just empty

Running on E

Sipping on air

Believe me

You don't want to see a future with no children

A "kid" is a baby goat

But they're more like sheep

convinced that they must follow to fit in with the heap

of shit

that comes their way

from the time they are born into this world

You hear what I say? In this world

Where Shepherds, wolves, it's all the same in this world where we wear the oppressors name

In this world

where they try to keep us locked up

But What's the missing key?

It's in the minds of our Young people dying in the streets

We gotta save our youth

We have to show them that they are the tools

Teach them there is no use looking outside of self

cause the power is in YOU.

We gotta save our youth

We gotta save the future

the tomorrow that seems so distant from today

yet sitting right here in front of our face

In Brownsville

barely able to sit still

but for this moment sitting right next to me

writing the beginnings of a poem

based on his experience

with police brutality.

We gotta save our youth!

BEFORE HE WAS THEO

Before he was Theo, he was J.R.

"J.R" two letters that spelled,

"Pain in my ass"

From years 8 until the present

and for a long time I resented the fact that he looked just like our father

But now he has grown into his own man

He loves basketball, trap music, writes cursive with his left hand

These are not the facts you would learn about him

You would never see a photo of his recent graduation from Discovery High gracing the front page

You would never know that he still lived life like it was worth living

despite this crazy day and age

They would have neglected to say

that he went to church every Sunday

and occasionally took our mother out on dates

My little Brother is not a saint

but he is so beautiful it's GODLIKE

and it is far from his time

with all these Black Brothers dying, I can't help but think about mine one of my biggest supporters, one of the only men I've ever loved

What lies would thy defend?

What portrait would they have to paint of him?

Would they go so far as to plant a weapon?

While reading about the next young thug to die

you would never realize that he fell in love with his high school sweetheart and for years they were just best friends

How many Theos, Travyions, Erics, and Alstons we gotta lose before this slaughter of our men comes to an end?

If God Forbid, I ever got that call

and they just took everything away,

music, his love of basketball

because his skin was too dark in the midst of it all

I wonder if they would make sure the world knew

That he had the softest smile any beautiful Black Man could have

Would they bother to tell the world that they always said he looked up to me?

But in all honesty, he was my hero

He was Blade slaying stereotypes and day walking in the light

He was Neo, unplugged from the matrix and staying focused on his goals

He was Iron man, filthy rich with melanated sun kissed skin

He was Green Lantern but he never needed a ring because all the supernatural minerals already existed within him

He is my hero

But they would say "young drug dealer killed by cop today"

You would hear about that time he got pulled over

you would hear that he frequently smoked marijuana

But you would never hear the breaking heart of my mama

Because that heart beats in a negro woman's chest

and it was just another colored boy who was laid to rest

I pray, I pray my family is never put to that test

I pray I never get that call

I pray you never have to scroll past another black body bleeding on the pavement

I pray you never have to hear another ignorant, racist statement

I pray for every family who had to watch as their hero; their brother, father, or son

was dismantled for the world to see

I pray for every Theo

in every shade of beautiful brown skin who has to walk through these blackened streets

I pray for any man in blue who dares to point and shoot

Because if you touch a hair on that Black Man's head

we coming for you

I pray for my people

who are grieving

who are angered

who are scared

I pray for my beautiful Black Heroes

I pray that they know

You are valued by us,

your sisters

Despite the slander to justify your murders

despite the attempts of the world to devalue you

despite the defamation of character

We have always known,

that your life MATTERS.

DEAR PHILLY

9/21/2016

I am sorry I haven't wrote you a letter in a while. It isn't because I didn't want to. Things have just been crazy for me. I almost feel guilty admitting my hardships while imagining what you are going through on Rikers. But it's true, I didn't know where I was going to go and was blessed to find a spot that I could quickly move into. Only two friends showed up to help. I drove a uhaul truck for the first time and had to leave a couple things that I thought were important to me but I detached from everything that wasn't absolutely necessary. It was a hard move but I'm proud of myself.

I now live in Flatbush, Brooklyn with a woman I barely know, and I am convinced she might be a little touched the more I get to know her. But the space seems safe for the moment and that is all that matters. I am so grateful.

I also started a new job teaching poetry to middle school students in East New York. It has been the highlight of my life being able to teach young boys and girls how to express themselves through poetry. It makes me feel like I am actually doing something that matters...I hope they appreciate my class as much as I appreciate having the opportunity to teach them.

In your letters you reference LOVE so often that it makes me hopeful that love still exists. I truly believe that we all deserve a love that is patient, kind, and everlasting no matter what we've done. I say that because I've done bad things...I've done things I am not proud of but I still believe that one day I might find a love that is mine all mine.

I am actually crying and feeling down on myself as I write this letter to you. I feel guilt, shame, and pain. I cannot sleep with my heart so heavy. But when I remember your words and your faith in love...it gives me faith too...faith that my dream of having a child one day will come true.

I apologize for typing this letter instead of sending you a handwritten one. I just needed to write back to you and let you know you are not forgotten. I will continue to write to you and keep in contact. Please use my new address when replying so I can receive your letters. And thank you so much for keeping faith alive in LOVE. I don't know how, I don't know when, but your faith refueled mine and I truly believe OUR dreams will come true and LOVE WILL PREVAIL.

Sincerely,

Relle the Poet

P.S

Isn't it so ironic how I thought I was encouraging you with my words and it was actually YOU who inspired ME with yours? Can't wait for your next letter!

FOR THE RIKERS BOYS

You gotta keep your head up prince, you are more than they say you are.

You gotta keep your head up king, your mind will get you far.

You gotta keep your head up brother, look your demons right in the eye

and keep your head up now, never let your spirit die.

Take a look around, tell me what do you see?

Has this world been any good to you or me?

I know I'm standing here seemingly shackle free,

While y'all sitting there under tight lock and key

I've also been a prisoner with face pressed on cold concrete

I know most of the time our efforts seem so obsolete

What happens when we all stop trying, stop caring, stop living?

This is not a game, if it is we sure ain't winning.

I say we as in us, one collective unit.

We fight our insides and wonder why we always going through it

This whole system is broken, every piece is corrupt

I know these words as adhesive will never be enough

But you have to know how important it is to keep your head up.

Keep your head up and eyes faced towards the sky

When they give you darkness and water, grow and continue to rise

Like the rose from the soil, covered in dirt you find life

I'm saying you can make a difference in this ongoing fight

This battle against our people involving weapons, fists, words,

and one messed up mentality that's infected the whole world.

They're the ones that sick, but the symptoms affect all of us

King I know your crown is heavy but please keep your head up.

You are caterpillars

Not soft but full of potential

I know you feel caged right now but you have something special

Think of these bars as the walls of your natural cocoon

When they thought you were finished, just tell them stay tuned

You are evolving, undergoing a kind of transformation

If they don't believe tell them ask the old you for confirmation

This body is temporary, break it down, liquify, never stay tied to your past

Strengthen and focus your mind.

Emerge from this place a brand new butterfly.

You better act like you know who you are and walk with some pride

Always remember to keep your heads up high.

You gotta keep your head up prince, you are more than they say you are.

You gotta keep your head up king, your mind will get you far.

You gotta keep your head up brother, look your demons right in the eye

and keep your head up now, never let your spirit die.

Cause one day you will take flight, just keep your head up!

THE SECRET OF THE NYLON POOL

a short story

Every family experiences their share of madness. Every auntie, cousin, sister, mom, well virtually every woman in my family can give you a tongue lashing you will never forget. And the men are usually mild tempered...until you get them angry.

This year we put all our differences aside for a big christmas vacation in Tobago. Those of us who had moved to the states years ago traveled by plane from Atlanta, Florida, and New York City to join those who chose to stay in our original home, Trinidad. Once we all met up at Grandmother's house in Arouca we loaded three cars and headed down the narrow roads leading to the ferry that sailed daily to Tobago.

I would never forget that ferry ride. Everyone took turns spilling their guts into barf bags.The smell of sea water and vomit filled my nose for five long hours before we finally reached the small island of Tobago.

As we drove from the ferry terminal up to our luxurious 10 bedroom villa in Black Rock, Tobago, a sense of excitement and nostalgia began swelling in the pit of my stomach. I was always the sentimental one in the family and simply remembering all the memories of vacations in Trinidad as a child brought tears to my eyes. So many memories about the land of my birth flooded back to me especially the ones of my grandfather who passed away just a couple years ago. I smiled at the thought of my hero.

That first night in Tobago was nothing short of magical. No one argued. No one was shouting and Grandmother kept her complaints to a minimal, only being just a little bit miserable, for the

117

sake of christmas of course.

There was a feast prepared for dinner and laid out on the large deck that overlooked the pool and the many palm trees swaying with the cool evening breeze. After I helped myself to two full servings of everything and finished off a healthy piece of rum cake for dessert, I was too full to do anything but sit there and rub my belly, comforted by the chatter of a family reunited. Tomorrow we would wake up early, drive to the beach and visit the mysterious Nylon Pool.

————

After shouts of "Get ready, we leaving in five minutes!", a couple kicks, and several threats to leave me, I finally rolled out of my large comfy bed and moved with sloth-like speed towards the bathroom. I brushed my teeth, dragged on a one-piece bathing suit that sensually exposed the skin of my belly and back but was tasteful enough to wear around the family, and pulled my locs into a ponytail. There, I was ready to go.

Three cars drove down to Pigeon Point where we would board yet another boat (this one much smaller than the ferry) and ride out to the middle of the ocean to a special place called, The Nylon Pool.

I was worried about Mommy as she struggled with her bad knees and hips into the rocking boat. Grandmother followed swiftly behind insisting, "I'm not as cripple as you Smallie!" My mother huffed, getting her bearings in the steady moving boat and ignoring the insult. Once all 13 of us piled in we were off. I just hoped there would be no more vomiting!

We enjoyed five minutes of nothing but white-blue waters, cloud free skies, and scenic views of the beautiful beach before our sailor Michael began his announcements.

"Here we are at the Buccoo Reef," he exclaimed

enthusiastically, as I'm sure he had many times before.

"You will find here many different species of coral and tropical fish. For instance, we have what we call the Deadman Finger. We call it that for the obvious reasons. Look closely and you can see some are brown and some are grey. When the Deadman is brown he is awake, and when he is grey, he is asleep." We listened intently to his voice and looked through the glass at the bottom of the boat to catch a glimpse of all the Dead men.

As we sailed through the Buccoo Reef and further into the ocean I began to feel nauseous. I rubbed my stomach and closed my eyes hoping the vomit would not come.

"You ok sis?" I turned to see my older sister's concerned eyes staring at me.

"I'm alright. Just feeling a little seasick ya know?" I gave her a weak smile to add more confidence to my words.

"Trust me, I feel you," she said, rubbing her own tummy. We both laughed until the sailor slowed the boat and quieted everyone with another announcement.

"We have arrived at the Nylon Pool. Here you will notice not only the difference in the shallow water, but after bathing in this majestic place you will begin to feel it's mystical properties. It is said that anyone who bathes in these waters will shed years off their life and children will stay forever young!" Some laughter erupted in the boat as the old wives tale continued.

"Everyone out the boat and into the pool. Don't worry, it's very shallow. Be sure to use the crushed coral that lines the bottom of the pool to exfoliate your skin. It's better than a spa!" There was more laughter at this last comment as the sailor Michael flashed us his gold tooth smile and we all proceeded to help Mommy out of the boat.

———

It seemed like we bathed for hours in those mystical waters. I was a little timid at first to rub my skin with the sand at the bottom of the ocean floor like Micheal suggested but once I saw everyone else doing it, I just followed suit. I couldn't believe how good it felt on my skin. Everywhere I had impurities, they were washed away and cleansed. I no longer felt any discomfort. I didn't feel any worries. I didn't feel any fears. Before long I wasn't even aware of all the people around me rubbing their own skin with the special sand and splashing in the magical waters. I only heard the wind whispering in my ear telling me that everything would be ok. It almost sounded like the voice of my grandfather soothing and comforting me. And when I closed my eyes and listened more intently I could hear the voice of my Tanti Edna who was also taken away from us by cancer. I felt a euphoria I had never experienced in my life before and instinctively I opened my mouth and began swallowing the sea water in big gulps. After a few moments of drinking the water as if it were wine, I heard a voice. This time it wasn't the wind but the voice of someone right here with me.

"Hello child" The voice belonged to my Tanti Edna. I looked up and smiled at her, wanting to throw my arms around her thin frame but something deep inside steadied me and allowed me to receive her message.

"You and your sister are very special. You are the chosen ones. This thing that has attacked us is no cancer as they say, but a curse that has been placed on us by an evil obeah woman centuries ago. Now is your time. You and your sister must pay her a visit and say the words that will drive her mad and reverse the spell."

I stood stunned. What the hell was she talking about? I know I felt high from the magic water and all that but this was a little much for me.

"I know you carry life inside you," Tanti said as if she could hear the doubt in my thoughts.

"But how? I haven't told anyone yet that I am pregnant," I

said.

"I can see right through you child. I see things that normal eyes cannot see. And soon you will too. Your grandfather will visit you and your sister tomorrow at midnight with the instructions on how to break the curse. And don't worry about a thing. You are carrying a true warrior inside you."

———————

I was awakened by the clenching feeling of my own gut attempting to regurgitate gallons of seawater that I had ingested earlier that day. I had no idea what time it was or how I got back in my bed from the Nylon pool but here I was rushing to one of the many toilets in our villa so I could throw up the magic water I had foolishly drank. What was I thinking?

"Sis?!" I was still blowing chunks in the downstairs bathroom near the pool when I heard my sister calling out to me.

"So you swallowed the water too?" She eyed me suspiciously as I straightened up and wiped my mouth.

"Did you...Did you see anything strange while we were out there in the Nylon Pool?" I asked her.

"Yeah I saw some crazy shit! I can't even remember how we got back from the beach. I gotta stop smoking!" We both laughed as my sister rubbed the side of her head with both hands and I rubbed my still upset tummy. We both couldn't believe what we saw.

We decided we would do some investigating and ask different members of the family what happened after we got to the Nylon Pool. They all said the same thing. We swam and played in the pool and got back in the boat, bought curry crab and dumplings on the way back to the villa and both me and my sis went straight to sleep.

"I wonder if it was hard labor yall was doing the way yall was sleeping," said Grandmother as she peered over her reading glasses to see better. At that last comment my sister decided the weed she bought must have been really strong and I thought, maybe it was just a dream after all.

———

The next morning I could hear Mommy whimpering from her master bedroom all the way down the hall. Her bedroom door was closed, so was mine. Even my eyes were closed but somehow I could hear her soft cries of discomfort. I was by her side in a flash. My body felt so strong and limber, like I could reach any destination within seconds no matter how far away I was.

"What's wrong?," I asked as I kneeled down beside her bed.

"My leg. It's swollen from all that struggling at the beach. It hurts so bad!" I looked down at my mother's leg and noticed it was swollen to the point where it was three times it's normal size. Tears welled up in my eyes. I felt so angry and helpless. My mother should never feel this pain. She's a good woman!

A few of my tears dripped from my face onto her swollen skin. I raised my hand to wipe the tears away but instead placed my palm right on her leg. I felt the heat rising in me as I channelled healing energy into her. I felt that euphoric floating feeling again. Like I was back at the Nylon Pool surrounded by white-blue waters, listening to the calming song of the wind. I closed my eyes submitting to the power I wasn't even sure I had.

Suddenly I felt my mom shift. She was no longer crying. She sat up slowly in the bed and gently removed my hand from her leg. The swelling had visibly improved.

"That felt great! You getting real good at those massages..." She eyed me suspiciously for a moment before smiling and saying "Come do my neck, I have a kink right here on the side everytime I turn to the left!"

We both laughed as I stood up and placed my hands on her

neck.

———

At breakfast I wanted to tell my Sis how I had healed mommy but I didn't get a chance. Grandmother made fresh sweetbread, sorrell, and scrambled eggs while everyone enjoyed the beauty of the morning sun on the large deck.

Mommy came practically dancing into the dining area with fresh clothes and powder on her chest, a sure sign that she had just bathe.

"Gyal, ya massage worked wonders! That plus the bathe in the Nylon Pool have me feeling like I loss the ten years fah true!"

We all laughed and beamed at my Mommy who really did look ten years younger and walked around like she never needed the knee or the hip replacement surgery.

My sister, though overjoyed, eyed me for a moment letting me know she was wondering the same thing I was.

After filling our plates with slices of sweetbread, Trinidad cheese (which I've heard is just cheddar), and scrambled eggs we took our places opposite each other at the long rectangular table in the middle of the deck.

"So how you feel about a midnight dip in the pool tonight?" She asked without looking up from her food. I simply nodded because my mouth was full but I knew she could feel me agreeing.

———

That night I slipped on a mismatched two piece bathing suit and headed down to the pool at 11:55pm. I didn't tell my little cousin or my aunties who loved to swim, because I just wanted it to be me and my sis. I knew it had to be.

My sis was already downstairs dipping her feet in the water

and staring up at the moon when I approached her.

"You think Grandfather will really come to us tonight, like Tanti Edna did?" I asked her. My voice sounded small. Just like it did when we were children.

"I am already here." My sister's head turned towards me and her eyes were tinted with gray, just like Grandfather's was before he died. And just like Tanti Edna.

My Grandfather's voice continued to channel through my sister's mouth.

"Your sister is the vessel for your ancestors to flow through. Her body is strong and she is the first born grandchild to the first born daughter. You my child are also special. Your power lies in your compassion and your words. You can heal the world or you can inflict great damage. You both must travel to Laventille and visit the grave where the Obeah woman is buried. Repeat these words over her grave while your sister channels the power of every warrior our family has ever known and the curse will surely be broken,

Deadman fingers brown and gray

awake or asleep the corals sway

Be with me, ancestors here and now I say

our curse will be broken today!"

———

I woke up again in my bed drenched in sweat with no recollection of how I got there. But this time I was sure it wasn't a dream. I remembered every word my Grandfather said and most importantly, I knew what I had to do.

———

The days past by mechanically. For christmas both my sister

and I got golden rings from our Grandmother. No one paid attention to the way we entered rooms as suddenly as well left them or the fact that Mommy had not used her walker or complained of pain in her legs since that day I healed her. Everyone was happy and soon we would all be free of the curse.

On the last day we packed up what was left of the food from our stay and all our luggage into the three cars. I was sad to leave the gorgeous villa behind but I knew there was work to be done.

The night before I dreamed that an army of Deadman Fingers had come alive and walked right out of the sea called by the magic that now dwell within my sister and I. The bubbling power beneath my skin was making me anxious.

The ferry ride itself was short and smooth and before we knew it we were back in Trinidad unloading all three cars in front of Grandmother's house.

"Tonight," my sister said as she passed me by and carried a large box of food items into the kitchen. She didn't have to say anymore, I knew what she meant.

————

We didn't tell anyone where we were going that night. But still, Grandmother's house was restless most likely with our nervous and powerful energy in the air. Before leaving my sister sat us down and we drank some tea, closed our eyes, and thought of the peace we found in Tobago to settle our minds. I imagined the sun shining down on my face as I gave myself to the waters of the Nylon pool. My sister later told me she felt the moon's rays helping her connect to all those that came before us. The entire house fell quiet after that, a signal that it was time.

The travel to Laventille took all of ten minutes by foot. Silently we flashed from town to town blending with the night, our feet moving faster than our minds could even think. I wouldn't allow myself to submit to fear but I held my belly as we traveled praying that the life I carried would be safe during this battle. I would trade even my own to protect it.

We automatically knew where to go. The evil energy poured from a dark and dreary cemetery practically calling our name.

"You ready?" my sister asked me as we slowed our pace and approached the den of graves.

"I know this is gonna sound mad cheesy...But I'm pretty sure we were born ready sis," I said in the most confident voice I could muster.

We looked at each other and smiled before focusing our attention back towards the cemetery and eventually entering the darkness.

Finding the right grave wasn't as easy as we thought. We searched for what seemed like an eternity (more like a couple hours) before coming across an unmarked slab jutting awkwardly out of the ground. We must have walked past it a couple times before noticing it was an unmarked grave.

"This is it. I can feel it," my sister said. I felt her energy rising as she prepared to channel our ancestors and begin the breaking of the curse. I started preparing myself, repeating the words over and over in my head, placing a hand on my tummy.

"So you've come foolish girls," screeched a voice that seemed to come from the pits of hell right below our feet. At least I thought it was coming from under us, until I turned to my sister and saw that her eyes were bloodshot red and suddenly something seemed very ominous about her.

"You opened yourself right up to me! And now I can use that precious baby of yours to regain life back into the physical realm", the evil wench spat these words right at my stomach laughing maniacally.

"Never!," I cried, backing away slowly from my sister's body unsure what to do. I tried to remember the words that would break the curse but my mind was frozen with fear for my unborn child.

"SIS! Remember your power! Remember your words," my sister's voice returned for a brief moment as she struggled with the witch to regain control over her body.

In that moment I felt a strong kick in my stomach for the first time I felt my baby move and I knew there was no way I was going to let the witch continue wreaking havoc on my family and I damn sure wasn't letting anyone touch my baby!

"Deadman fingers brown and gray," I began. "Awake or asleep the corals sway"

"HA! You think your silly poems can defeat me!," The nameless obeah woman shouted as she wrestled my sister for control over her body.

"Be with me, ancestors here and now I say!," I shouted. At these words I felt the presence of my Grandfather, Uncle Kenrick, Uncle Ricky, Auntie Mona, Tanti Enda, Tanti Ellie, Great Grandma Sarah, and all who came before me suddenly behind me, pushing me forward and giving my words power.

"Our curse will be broken today!," I shouted these last words as if they were swords coming full force at the enemy.

"It's working sis, keep going!," My sister said finally beginning to regain control of her own body.

"Deadman fingers brown and gray

awake or asleep the corals sway

Be with me, ancestors here and now I say

our curse will be broken today!"

I spoke these words over and over again. I spoke the words until my mouth became dry and my tongue was tired. I spoke the words as if it was I who wrote them a thousand years ago just for this moment. I spoke the words as if our lives depended on it. I spoke the words with both the power of my ancestors and the power of my unborn child. The future and the past both spoke through me that night. And thus, the curse was broken.

––––––––––

When I left Trinidad and returned to New York after the holiday I noticed my "powers" weakening the further and further I got from the island. I once again had that familiar feeling that maybe it was all just a dream. I know it wasn't but it's still hard to believe what my sister and I had accomplished that night.

I got home in the late afternoon the day after New Years and called my Mommy who had returned to her home in Atlanta.

"Hey Mommy, how you feeling?," I said so happy to hear her voice.

"I feel great! I'm telling you those rub downs you gave me were like magic. Plus I think that good old Trini air was good for me. I might make sure to go back every year, especially now that your sister decide she staying," My mother said.

A sad smile crept across my face. I was happy my sister decided to stay in Trinidad and keep her powers. We needed someone to watch over and protect our family even with the curse gone.

"There is something I been meaning to ask you Mommy. I just felt so powerful after dipping in the Nylon Pool that day. Do you think the stories are true about the mystical properties of the water?"

"Chile I think whatever powers you gain from the Nylon Pool

is the same powers you had all along. Sometimes you just need a reminder of where you come from so you can never ever forget who you are. You are my child. That's where you get your power from, not no pool! Anyway I tired from all that traveling so I gone!"

I laughed and said, "You right Mommy. Go now and get some rest. I love you."

———

That summer I gave birth to twins. I brought a beautiful baby girl and boy into this world. The day they were born I felt even more powerful than the day we broke the curse. I held them both in my arms with tears of joy streaming down my face thinking about how I'll take them to the Nylon Pool when they get just a little older.

ABOUT THE AUTHOR

Jherelle Benn, better known as Relle the Poet, started writing at a young age. Once she reached adulthood she saw the way her words impacted people. It became her purpose to share her gift on stages at open mics, artist showcases, the subways, and during freestyle sessions just about anywhere.

After graduating from Brooklyn College in June 2016, Relle continued to pursue a career in writing by teaching, hosting literary workshops, and uplifting the people in her community through the art of poetry.

Born in Trinidad and Tobago and raised in Brooklyn NY, Relle incorporates a blend of spicy Caribbean and gritty New York City culture to create a unique voice in her writing.

She now lives in Georgia raising her twin boy and girl.